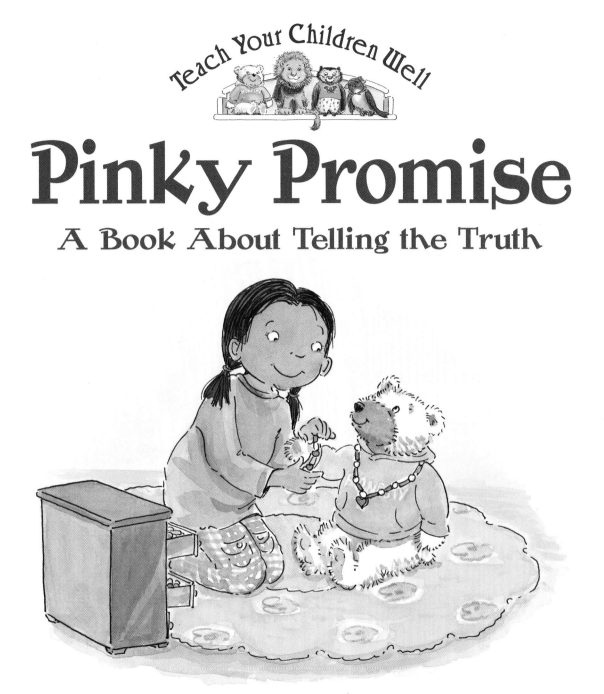

Teach Your Children Well

Pinky Promise

A Book About Telling the Truth

By Vanita Braver, MD · Illustrated by Cary Pillo

Child & Family Press   Washington, DC

Child & Family Press is an imprint of the Child Welfare League of America. The Child Welfare League of America is the nation's oldest and largest membership-based child welfare organization. We are committed to engaging people everywhere in promoting the well-being of children, youth, and their families, and protecting every child from harm. All proceeds from the sale of this book benefit CWLA's programs in behalf of children and families.

CHILD WELFARE LEAGUE OF AMERICA, INC.
HEADQUARTERS
440 First Street, NW, Third Floor, Washington, DC 20001-2085
www.cwla.org
E-mail: books@cwla.org

Text design by Amy Alick Perich
Edited by Tegan A. Culler

Printing
10 9 8 7 6 5 4 3 2

ISBN# 0-87868-893-5
Printed in the United States of America

Library of Congress Cataloging-in-Publications Data
Braver, Vanita.
  Pinky promise : a book about telling the truth / by Vanita Braver ; illustrated by Cary Pillo.
      p. cm. — (Teach your children well)
  Summary: When five-year-old Madison drops her mother's expensive camera on the floor she is afraid to tell the truth about what happened, but she soon discovers that lying only makes her feel worse.
  ISBN 0-87868-893-5 (alk. paper)
  [1. Honesty—Fiction. 2. Conduct of life—Fiction.] I. Pillo, Cary, ill. II. Title.
  PZ7.B73795Pi 2004
  [E]—dc21   2004018414

Dedication

To my wonderful children, Alyssa, India, and Samantha, and my amazing husband, Joel, with boundless love and gratitude for your support and encouragement.

To my loving parents, who have always been a source of inspiration to me. To my Bonnie Brae family with much warmth and affection.

Acknowledgments

I would like to acknowledge Karen Pinzolo; Sangeeta Tyerech; Kathy Lewis; Anne Picciano; Joan Elste; Karen Gruenberg; Marlene Browne; Liesa Abrams; Central School Faculty and students in Warren, NJ; and my brilliant CWLA team—Tegan Culler, Eve Malakoff-Klein, and Yelba Quinn. Thanks for sharing in my dream and for all your wisdom.

"Here comes Honesty!" said Madison, tossing her favorite bear at her best friend, Emily.

Emily ducked, and Honesty crashed into Madison's new bead kit.

"What are you two up to?" called Madison's mother, hearing the noise from Madison's room.

"Nothing, Mom. We're just playing with my stuffed animals."

"Well, don't make a mess in there," said her mother.

"We won't," giggled the girls, eyeing the beads spread across the floor.

"Wow, look at these great beads. What cool colors!" exclaimed Emily. "Let's make some jewelry. I bet we have enough to make necklaces and bracelets. Can I keep what I make?"

"Of course," said Madison. She grabbed some of the red heart-shaped beads along with some tiny gold ones.

"Can I use some of those heart-shaped ones, too? I'm going to mix them with these," said Emily, holding out a handful of pearly white beads.

"Sure, there are plenty. Those will look pretty together," replied Madison.

Slowly, the girls strung one bead after another onto the strings. When they were finished, they carefully tied a knot in each and tried them on.

"I like your necklace better," said Emily.

"Well, I like your bracelet better," declared Madison.

"Trade!" they shouted in unison.

"Wow! You girls have outdone yourselves," said Madison's mom as the girls entered the family room. "Those are beautiful."

"Oh, Mommy, please take a picture of us with our new jewelry!" begged Madison.

"Okay, in just a minute. I have to put this laundry away." Madison's mom carried the laundry basket up the stairs.

"I know how to use my mom's camera," bragged Madison, as she took the
camera out of the cabinet. "All you do is look through here and press this
button. Stand over there and say 'cheese.'"

"No, let's just wait for your mom to take a picture of us together," said Emily.

"All right," agreed Madison.

But just as Madison was placing the camera back into the case, it slipped from her hand and fell to the floor with a loud thud!

"Oh no!" gasped Emily. "I hope you didn't break it."

Madison picked up the camera and tried to press down the button, but the button wouldn't work.

"I *did* break it!" she cried. "My mom's going to be really mad."

"Uh oh!" said Emily. "I think I hear her coming."

Madison quickly put the camera back in the cabinet.

"Is everything all right?" Madison's mother asked. "I thought I heard a noise."

"Everything's fine," squeaked Madison. Her face turned bright red.

"Let's take that picture now." Madison's mom opened the cabinet. "You two look so cute."

"That's okay, Mom." Madison bit her fingernails. "We don't really want to have our picture taken anymore."

"Oh, it will only take a second. Now stand over there and smile." Madison's mom pointed across the room. "On the count of three, say 'cheese' and give me the best smile you've got! One, two, and three!" she counted.

Nothing happened.

"That's odd," said Madison's mother. "The button won't press. It was fine last week. I wonder why it's not working?"

"I don't know," said Madison. "*I* didn't touch it."

"Madison!" whispered Emily. "You just lied to your mom."

Madison stared down at the floor.

That night during dinner, Madison could hardly look at her parents. She played with the food on her plate instead.

"Is something wrong, Sweetie?" asked her father. "You're not eating your supper, and you're awfully quiet."

"It's nothing, Dad," mumbled Madison.

Then Madison's mother told her father about the camera. Madison's belly began to ache.

"That's an expensive camera," he said. "How did it break?"

"I have no idea. It was working fine the other day," answered her mother.

Madison asked to be excused. She quickly left the table and went up to her room. Her stomach really hurt now, so she lay down on her bed. Looking up, Madison noticed Honesty Bear staring down at her from the shelf. "What am I going to do?" she asked him.

Madison reached for Honesty and hugged him tight.

She went back to the kitchen to help clear the table. Her father was loading the dishwasher.

"After you do your homework, I'll go over it with you," he said. Then he saw the look on Madison's face. "What's the matter, Honey?" he asked. "Aren't you feeling well?"

Madison's voice quivered as she asked, "Dad, if somebody did something wrong and then lied about it, what should they do?"

"What do *you* think somebody should do?" asked Madison's father, raising his eyebrows.

"Tell the truth," sighed Madison.

"That's a good start," agreed her father. "Any other thoughts?"

"Say you're sorry," whispered Madison.

Her father placed the last plate in the dishwasher and patted Madison on the back.

Madison walked slowly into the family room, where her mom was working on the computer.

"Mommy, I have something to tell you," said Madison. She began to cry as she spoke. "I accidentally dropped the camera when Emily was over. I'm sorry I didn't tell the truth before."

"So that's what happened to it," said Madison's mom. "Why didn't you tell me earlier?"

"I was afraid I'd get in trouble," whispered Madison.

"Well, what do you think we should do about it?" asked her mother, putting her arm around Madison and handing her a tissue.

"I don't know, Mommy. I won't ever lie again," said Madison. Then she slowly extended her right pinky.

"I hope not. I'm glad you told me the truth." Her mother hooked her pinky around Madison's.

"Pinky Promise," they said together.

"Does that mean I'm not in trouble?" asked Madison.

Madison's mom laughed. "No, you're not in trouble. I think you've suffered enough. You didn't seem like yourself all evening. I thought you were coming down with something."

Madison felt a lot better now that she'd told the truth. Her belly stopped hurting and she started to get hungry again. She sat at the kitchen table and did her homework. When she was finished, she made herself a snack.

That night, as Madison's mom tucked her into bed, she said, "Madison, I want to thank you for telling me the truth. I know it wasn't easy to admit you did something wrong."

"I'm glad I told you, Mommy. I feel much better," smiled Madison.

"Have a good night. I love you," said Madison's mom, tucking her into bed.

"I love you too, Mommy. Good night," replied Madison, as she gave her mom a kiss.

Madison's mom left the room, and all was quiet. Madison closed her eyes once and then slowly peeped them open again. She smiled as she saw Honesty Bear scamper down off the shelf. He cuddled next to her.

As Madison was drifting off to sleep, Honesty whispered into her ear, "Telling a lie makes us feel bad inside. You should feel good about yourself—especially when you are honest."

With that, Madison fell sound asleep.